THE WISDOM

of the

ZEN MASTERS

TIMOTHY FREKE

First published in 1998 by Journey Editions, an imprint of
Periplus Editions (HK) Ltd., with editorial offices at
153 Milk Street, Boston, Massachusetts 02109.

Distributed by:
USA
Charles E. Tuttle Co., Inc. RR 1 Box 231-5
North Clarendon, VT 05759
Tel.: (802) 773-8930 Fax.: (802) 773-6993

Japan
Tuttle Shokai Ltd. 1-21-13, Seki
Tama-ku, Kawasaki-shi
Kanagawa-ken 214
Japan
Tel.: (044) 833-0225 Fax.: (044) 822-0413

Southeast Asia
Berkeley Books Pte. Ltd. 5 Little Road #08-01
Singapore 536983
Tel.: (65) 280-3320 Fax.: (65) 280-6290

ISBN 1-885203-53-5
The Catalog Card Number is on file with
the Library of Congress

Printed in Hong Kong

CONTENTS

Introduction

The founder of Buddhism was a 6th-century BC Indian sage, known by the title "Buddha" or "Awakened One." The masters who succeeded him are known as the Patriarchs. The 28th Indian Patriarch was called Bodhidharma, whose name means "Knower of the Way." In the 6th century AD he traveled to China where he inspired a radical school of Buddhism known as "Chan." In the 12th century AD this reached Japan and acquired the familiar name "Zen."

This collection of Zen quotations is a conundrum, because Zen is beyond words. Zen is a direct experience of the way things are. Zen is a personal journey to enlightenment, at the end of which the seeker finds he is not a person and there was no journey. Zen is knowing the mind, without using thought. Zen is living one's life by letting it live itself. Zen is choosing to have no preferences. Zen is becoming extraordinary by being nothing special. To understand Zen is to embrace paradox – to find the oneness that contains all opposites. The Zen masters are sacrilegious and outrageous. They ridicule

Zen teachings and each other because enlightenment is not something that can be taught, but only directly experienced for oneself. Zen cannot be understood by the mind, because it is about becoming aware of the mind itself. These thoughts from the great Zen masters are not clever theories or philosophies, they are medicine. We suffer from the illness of the illusion separateness. We believe that the world is full of discrete things, when in fact it is all one interconnected whole. We experience ourselves as conscious skin-bags living a transitory mortal life, when in fact we are the eternal mind of the universe. Separateness is the sickness and Zen is the cure.

1. Buddha-nature

Zen teaches that we are not the transitory mortals we take ourselves to be. We are eternal Buddha-nature. Anything the mind thinks itself to be is just a thought in the mind. It is an illusion. Buddha-nature is the mind itself. The idea of who we are is a false self – our ego. It is like a cloud that obscures the empty sky of our essential Buddha-nature, that is our true identity. In the absence of this idea, we know ourselves to be the empty void of pure consciousness. We understand that all things, including our separate identities, are animated by one mind, and we are that. This is enlightenment.

The Buddha and all sentient beings
are nothing but expressions of the one
mind. There is nothing else.

HUANG-PO

> *Buddha-Nature, the Self of all beings, is the simple Truth. From Buddhas to insects, it is the seer, hearer, and mover.*
>
> BASSUI

66 Through endless ages, the mind has never changed. It has not lived or died, come or gone, gained or lost. It isn't pure or tainted, good or bad, past or future, true or false, male or female. It isn't reserved for monks or lay people, elders or youths, masters or idiots, the enlightened or the unenlightened.

It isn't bound by cause and effect and doesn't struggle for liberation. Like space, it has no form. You can't own it and you can't lose it. Mountains, rivers or walls can't impede it. But this mind is ineffable and difficult to experience. It is not the mind of the senses. So many are looking for this mind, yet it already animates their bodies. It is theirs, yet they don't realize it. 99

BODHIDHARMA

When master Tongxuan was asked
"Can you see someone else's mind with
one's own mind?" he replied "Can you see
another mind if you cannot see your own?"

Mind is the Buddha. There is no other
Buddha. There are no other Buddhas.
There are no other minds. Mind is pure,
bright, and empty, without having any
form or appearance at all. Using the
mind to think conceptually is missing
the essence and grasping the form.
The eternal Buddha is nothing
to do with attachment to form.

HUANG-PO

Those who seek the Buddha outside their
own minds are like children of rich
parents who have forgotten their home.

BASSUI

12

The light of Consciousness embraces the whole universe.

PAN-SHAN

66 Ikkyu visited a dying student and asked if he required his help. The man replied "I don't need anything. I am just going to the changeless." "If you think you are a something that can go anywhere, you still need my teachings," replied Ikkyu. 99

66 Master Bassui reduced the whole of Buddhist teachings to one phrase "Seeing one's own nature is Buddhahood." When asked how to see into one's own nature, master Bassui would reply "Now! Who is asking?" 99

66 A student asked master Bankei "How can I cure my terrible temper?" "Show it to me," demanded Bankei. "I can't just show it to you like that because it comes on unexpectedly," explained the student. Bankei replied "It is not your true nature, then. If it were it would be with you at all times." 99

> A deluded mind is hell.
> Without delusions,
> the mind is the country of the Buddhas.
> When the mind creates the idea of the mind,
> people are deluded and in hell.
> Those established on the path to Buddhahood
> don't use the mind to create the idea
> of the mind and so are always
> in the country of the Buddhas.

BODHIDHARMA

66 People are scared to empty their minds
fearing that they will be engulfed by the void.
What they don't realize is that
their own mind is the void. 99

HUANG-PO

66 Here is the unsophisticated Self –
your original face.
Here is the landscape of your birthplace –
bare and beautiful. 99

YUAN-WU

66 Worldly fools search for exotic masters,
not realizing that
their own mind is the master. 99

BODHIDHARMA

> Confused by thoughts,
> we experience duality in life.
> Unencumbered by ideas,
> the enlightened see the one Reality.
>
> HUI-NENG

> Only by accepting that the ego
> is a fabricated illusion do we walk
> the Buddha's Way.
>
> DOGEN

*A student who felt he had achieved
emptiness of mind boasted to his master,
"Now I have no idea."
The master replied, "Why stagger
about under the weight
of this concept 'no idea'?"*

ZEN TEACHING STORY

*A naïve student regarded
his master as a living Buddha
until one day the master sat down
on a needle and jumped up with
a yell of "ouch." The student was
disappointed and concluded
that the master could not be fully
enlightened after all. As the student
left the master remarked, "How sad.
If only he could realize that neither me,
nor the needle, nor the 'ouch'
have ever really existed."*

66 It is present everywhere.
There is nothing it does not contain.
However. only those who have previously
planted wisdom-seeds will be able
to continuously see it. **99**

DOGEN

" A student asked, "What is the mind?"
The master answered, "Mind is the Buddha."
The student said, "Thank you. Now I see."
The master replied, "Now that you see, I say the truth is
there is no mind and no Buddha."
The astonished student exclaimed, "Then why did you say
'The mind is the Buddha'?"
The master explained, "I had to stop the baby crying." "

ZEN TEACHING STORY

Let go of the idea "I exist."

IKKYU

11. The Zen Path

Enlightenment is a spontaneous realization of one's essential Buddha-nature. Enlightenment is not something one can get for oneself. It is the complete absence of the illusion of self. To chase enlightenment is to run in the opposite direction. Although enlightenment cannot be forced, by stilling the mind, opening the heart, cultivating humble acceptance, sincerity, and non-attachment, Zen students purify themselves of selfishness and so loosen the grip of the separate ego. Like clouds of confusion dispersing in an empty sky, when the illusion of the self is dispelled the natural clarity of enlightenment is revealed.

66 Understand now what you failed to understand
in past lives. In this life free this repeatedly born body.
Before they were enlightened, the ancient Buddhas were the
same as people today. Once enlightened, people today are
the same as the ancient Buddhas. 99

ROYA

THE **FOUR NOBLE TRUTHS**
TAUGHT BY THE BUDDHA

I. Life is suffering.

II. The origins of suffering is
selfish desire and attachment.

III. There is a way to stop suffering.

IV. This way is the Eightfold Path
Right Understanding;
Right Thinking;
Right Speech;
Right Attitude;
Right Livelihood;
Right Effort;
Right Mindfulness;
Right Concentration.

*Once you aspire to become enlightened,
even if your life takes you in many
different directions, the conditions
of your life all become a practical part
of achieving enlightenment.*

DOGEN

" A famous Chinese statesman and poet visited master Dorin and asked, "What is the deep meaning of Buddhism?" Dorin replied, "Don't do anything evil, only do good." The statesman exclaimed, "What? Even a three year old child could say this." Dorin answered, "A three year old child may be able to say it, but can an eighty year old man practice it?" "

ZEN TEACHING STORY

" For twenty years an old Chinese woman fed a monk while he meditated in the little hut she had built for him. One day she wondered if he had made any progress, so she employed a pleasure girl to visit the monk. Following the old woman's orders, the girl caressed the monk and seductively demanded, "Now what?" The monk answered, "Nothing is warm. Just an old tree growing from cold rocks in the winter." When the old woman heard this she exclaimed angrily, "I fed that fraud for twenty years, and he shows you no loving kindness! He needn't have been passionate, just a little compassion would have done." The old woman never fed the monk again. "

ZEN TEACHING STORY

The entire world is a doorway to freedom,
but people don't want to pass through.

HUIWU

The Way is not difficult for those
without preferences.

SENG-T'SAN

Students of the Way today have superficial aspirations and insufficient character. They don't think about the great mysteries of life and death. They are always going to teachers, but they don't get to the bottom of things. They are only concerned with their relationship to the teacher and how famous he is.

BASSUI

When studying Zen and seeking Buddhahood, don't see Buddhahood as the goal. If you do, it will become further away.

DOGEN

If you repent, you will receive invisible help from the enlightened ones. With thought and action you should confess to the Buddhas. This has the power to wither the root of error.

DOGEN

" Hakuin was admired for living a pure life until one day a young village girl became pregnant and claimed that he was the father. The villagers were angry. When the child was born they presented Hakuin with the baby and told him he must look after it because it was his. Hakuin replied, "Is that so?" and took in the child and cared for it. A year later the girl confessed that the real father was a village boy and the ashamed villagers went to Hakuin and asked for the child back, saying he was not the father. Hakuin said, "Is that so?" and gave up the baby. "

Consider the trees that allow the birds
to perch and fly away without calling
them to come or longing for them
not to leave. If your heart can be like
a tree you will be close to the Way.

LANGYA

I witness the worldly wasting their lives;
punishing themselves through
their endless craving;
seeking satisfaction but finding despair.
Their enjoyment of getting is only short lived.
One day in heavenly pleasure,
then ten days in hellish torment.
Shackled to the grindstone by their own hands.
Like monkeys snatching at moonlight on water,
they tumble into the swirling;
entranced by this drifting world of suffering.
I can't help myself caring.
I can't stop my tears falling.

RYOKAN

*The greatest gift to others
is to freely relinquish yourself.*

BODHIDHARMA

III. A Finger Pointing at the Moon

Zen teachings are like the word "silence" that breaks the silence in order to bring our attention to it. They fill the mind with ideas to bring to our attention the empty mind that contains them. Zen teachings are compared to a finger pointing at the moon. So that the student does not mistake the finger for the moon, Zen masters constantly undermine themselves and their teachings. They call the sutra scriptures "wastepaper," and famous masters "old windbags." Master Lin-chi called the Buddha himself a "privy hole!" This eccentric behavior reminds us that all that really matters is that we directly experienced the Truth for ourselves.

> **❝** I'd love to give you something helpful,
> but in Zen we don't have anything. **❞**
>
> ↓ IKKYU

A student asked
Master Zhengqin,
"What is the road
to Right Effort?"
He replied, "Where are
you coming from?"

66 If you use your mind to try and understand reality,
you will understand neither your mind nor reality.
If you try and understand reality without using your mind,
you will understand both your mind and reality. **99**

BODHIDHARMA

66 In the same way that insects can settle anywhere
but in the flames of a fire, so the limited mind
can relate to anything but transcendental wisdom. **99**

BAIZHANG

What is called the teaching
of the Buddha is not the teaching
of the Buddha.

DIAMOND SUTRA

Reality cannot be explained
by comparison, because there is
nothing to liken it to.

BAIZHANG

The Way is fundamentally the same for
everyone. Its essence is to awaken without
this being an achievement. Even saying
the word "awaken" creates waves on still
waters. This is even more true with
teachings and sayings. If you grasp the
leftovers you cannot hold to reality and
will end up cut off from the source.

BASSUI

The transcendental is unchanging.
If you point to it you turn away from it.

TONGAN ZHI

Don't search for truth.
Just stop having opinions.

SENG-T'SAN

Buddha-babble blocks the Way.

LKKYU

I have not heard of a single Buddha,
past or present, who has been
enlightened by sacred prayers
and scriptures.

BASSUI

66 All verbal teachings are just to cure an illness. Different illnesses require different cures. This is why sometimes it is said there is only Buddha and sometimes that there is no Buddha. True teachings cure the illness. If the cure works, the teachings are true. If they don't cure the illness, the teachings are false. True teachings are false if they create opinions. False teachings are true if they destroy delusions. The illness is an illusion anyway, so all the cures are also illusions. 99

BAIZHANG

66 Master Hogen asked a monk. "Look at this big old stone. Do you think it is inside or outside of your mind?" The monk replied. "According to Buddhist teachings. everything is a projection of the mind, so I conclude that it is inside my mind." Hogen commented. "Don't you get tired carrying around such a heavy stone." 99

66 A student asked master Bassui. "How can you discriminate between a true statement and a false statement?" He replied. "Whether a statement is true or false depends on the heart of the speaker not on the words he uses. Without meeting the person in question. it is impossible to tell." 99

66 A 16-year-old girl called Satsu soon became awakened after studying with Master Hakuin. One day her father found her in meditation while sitting on a box. "What are you doing?" he exclaimed. "There is a statue of the Buddha in that box." The young girl replied to her astonished father. "If there is any place where the Buddha does not exist – take me there." 99

When I'm through with thinking
I wander in the woods
gathering handfuls of flowers.

RYOKAN

" To benefit from reading the sutras you must
first awaken the mind that reads them. Formal study
is ultimately unhelpful. The wonderful nature of your mind,
unchanging through countless ages, is the essence of all the
sutras. To understand this essence listen to the call of frogs,
the billowing wind, the falling rain, all speaking the
wonderful language of the Essential Nature. Soaring birds,
swimming fish, flowing waters, passing clouds, are the wheel
of Essential Nature turning. If you hear the wordless sutra
once, the heavens will become sutras filled with golden
words, clear and obvious before you. "

BASSUI

*When Master Wensui was asked, "What is
the scripture in which all the Buddha's
teachings may be found?" He replied,
"It is continually being recited."*

IV. Meditation

The name "Zen" is derived from the Sanskrit word "dhyana" meaning "meditation." Through meditation Zen students still their thoughts and become aware of the empty mind that contains them. Just as the particles in a glass of muddy water settle to the bottom when the glass is no longer shaken and the water becomes transparent, so thoughts settle down when the mind is not agitated and consciousness becomes clear. But Zen is not meditation. Becoming a macho meditator who can sit in an upright posture for days on end is not Zen. It is just a new spiritual self. Zen is no-self.

> 66 When the mind is always empty, you journey
> from place to place in the country of the Buddhas.
> When the mind is always moving, you travel
> from one hell to the next hell. 99
>
> BODHIDHARMA

*Find the silence which
contains thoughts.*

HAKUIN

*Outwardly in the world
of good and evil,
yet without thoughts stirring the heart –
this is meditation.*

*Inwardly seeing one's
own true nature
and not being distracted from it –
this is meditation.*

HUI-NENG

*When you try to stop doing
to achieve being, this very effort
fills you with doing.*

SENG-T'SAN

> Meditation is the reservoir of wisdom,
> and the garden of bliss.
> Like pure water,
> it washes away the dust of desire.
> It is armor that protects from evil appetites.
> You may not have achieved the state of no-doer,
> but you are on your way towards enlightenment.
> When agitation rises like dust that obscures the sun,
> the rain may damp it down,
> the wind of intellectual insight may disperse it,
> but only meditation will remove for ever.

CHI-SHA DAISHI

“ Ma'tsu was living as an ascetic and practicing meditation. Master Huai Jang asked, "What are you doing?" Ma'tsu replied, "Trying to be a Buddha." Huai Jang picked up a stone and began rubbing it. "What are you doing?" asked Ma'tsu. Huai Jang replied, "I am trying to make a mirror." Ma'tsu said. "No amount of polishing will make a stone a mirror." Huai Jang said. "No amount of meditation will make you a Buddha." ”

A student once asked
master Rugan,
"What is your Buddhism?"
He replied, "Piling fresh fruit in
a basket without a bottom."

“ People perform a vast number of complex practices
hoping to gain spiritual merit as countless as the grains
of sand on the riverbed of the Ganges; but you are
essentially already perfect in every way. Don't try and
augment perfection with meaningless practice. If it's the
right occasion to perform them, let practices happen. When
the time has passed, let them stop. If you are not absolutely
sure that mind is the Buddha, and if you are attached to the
ideas of winning merit from spiritual practices, then your
thinking is misguided and not in harmony with the Way. To
practice complex spiritual practices is to progress step by
step; but the eternal Buddha is not a Buddha of progressive
stages. Just awaken to the one Mind, and there is absolutely
nothing to be attained. This is the real Buddha. ”

HUANG-PO

“ Trying to get rid of habits that derive from attachment
to form without having seen into your own nature,
is like trying to get rid of a dream while asleep.
The desire to dispel the dream is just part of the dream.
Knowing that it is a dream is also just part of the dream.
It doesn't matter how much you search for something
in a dream, you will never find it. ”

BASSUI

v. Be Here Now

Enlightenment can not happen in the future, but only here and now. Zen brings us into a complete appreciation of the moment, that is the only reality. Zen is found in the obvious. It is conscious ordinariness. It is experiencing the fullness of the senses, unlimited by the thinking mind. It is enjoying the everchanging richness of existence. It is wonderment in the face of the miracle of life. It is witnessing things as they are. It is being Buddha-nature – the presence that is always present.

You can't prevent time passing.
When something has passed,
why do thoughts still loiter?

RYOKAN

    Tsing-ping asked master T'sui-wei. "What is the
fundamental principle of Buddhism?" "I will tell you later
when there is no one else around." said the master. Later,
when they were alone, Tsing-ping again asked his question.
The master led his student out into the bamboo grove. but
he still said nothing. Tsing-ping pressed him for an answer.
T'sui-wei whispered. "Look how high these bamboos are!
And how short those over there!"

Here it is – right now. Start thinking
about it and you miss it.

HUANG-PO

A student asked, "What is Zen?"
The master answered, "It is right before
your eyes." The student asked, "So why
can't I see it?" The master answered,
"Because you have a 'me'." The student
asked, "If I no longer have the concept
'me', will I realize Zen?" The master
answered, "If there is no 'me'
who wants to realize Zen?"

ZEN TEACHING STORY

Kakua was the first Japanese to study
Zen in China. When he returned to
Japan the emperor asked him to instruct
him. Kakua stood silent and unmoving,
then he blew
a single note on a flute and left.

66 Buddhism has no room for special effort.
Just be ordinary and nothing special. Eat and drink,
then move your bowels and pass water, and when you're
tired go to sleep. Fools will find me ridiculous,
but the wise will understand. 99

LIN-CHI

>--<--0--<--<

66 A student once asked master Bassui,
"Are you saying that someone who sees his own nature
and is free from delusion is innocent of error,
even if he does something which breaks the Buddhist
precepts?" He replied, "If someone's actions come
from their essential nature, how could they
be breaking the precepts?" 99

>--<--0--<--<

66 A student once asked master Fenglin, "Do you enjoy sex
and money?" He answered, "Indeed yes." The astonished
student exclaimed, "But you are a spiritual teacher,
how come you enjoy sex and money."
Fenglin replied, "So few are truly grateful." 99

When master Puman was asked,
"What is your Buddhism?" he replied,
"What is here and now?"

When master Caoshan was asked,
"What is the meaning of Buddhism,"
he replied, "It is everywhere."

On the day that he died Master Tanzan
asked his assistant to send a number of
postcards, that all simply read "I am
leaving this world. There will be no further
announcements. Tanzan."

I haven't got any Buddhism.
I live by letting things happen.

DOGEN

Playing at love in the summer house,
a beautiful young girl and an old Zen monk;
passionate embraces and affectionate kisses
—this doesn't feel like hell to me!

IKKYU

I play in this world,
with this body, not thinking
about the world to come.

RYOKAN

The past has passed already.
The moment won't stay
for a moment.
The prepared for future never comes.

P'ANG YUN

VI. Enlightenment

In Zen the empty void of pure Consciousness is the absolute reality and the world of separate things is an illusion that is only relatively real. However, enlightenment is not rejecting one for the other. It is both and neither. In it there is no duality. As if a negative and positive combine to cancel each other out, the enlightened master is attached to neither form nor emptiness. Both are seen to be mere concepts. Reality is experienced directly. Things are what they are. No comment.

> *You have two eyes, to see both the relative and the absolute. Don't see through one only, for then you will be partially sighted.*
>
> BAIZHANG

THE **FIVE LEVELS** OF **ZEN**

Understanding the Absolute: The Oneness of Being is revealed: the primal source of the many appearances, beyond good and bad.

Understanding the Relative: Spontaneously going along with things, like an empty boat: open, detached, and free.

Understanding the Relative within the Absolute: Everywhere is pervaded by space: objects and senses are silent

Understanding the Absolute within the Relative: A reflection of the moon in water or an image in a mirror has no existence and so cannot be destroyed or leave any remnants.

Understanding that the Absolute and Relative are One: The Absolute is not emptiness and the relative is not substantial: no pushing away or opinion.

CAOSHAN

*When a student asked master Guangfan,
"What am I?" he replied, "What is there
in the entire universe that is not you?"*

*To follow the Way do not push away
anything, even sensual experiences
and thoughts. In fact, to accept them
completely is enlightenment.*

SENG-T'SAN

*As long as you remain in one extreme or
another you will never know Oneness.*

SENG-T'SAN

*When an ignorant person understands,
he become a saint. But when a saint
understands, he becomes an ignorant person.*

EKAI

The first stage of goodness is reached through the teaching that the mirroring consciousness of the present is your own Buddha. The next stage is to cease one's preoccupation with the mirroring consciousness of the present. The final stage is not to have any ideas about this.

BAIZHANG

Unfettered like a wafting mist
I give myself up
to where the wind wants me to be.

RYOKAN

> 66 When practitioners of Zen fail to transcend
> the world of their senses and thoughts, all they do has
> no value. Yet, when senses and thoughts are obliterated
> all the roads to universal mind are blocked and there is
> no entrance. The primal mind has to be recognized along
> with the senses and thoughts. It neither belongs to them
> nor is independent of them. Don't build your understanding
> on your senses and thoughts, yet don't look for the mind
> separate from your senses and thoughts. Don't attempt to
> grasp Reality by pushing away your senses and thoughts.
> Unobstructed freedom is to be neither attached
> nor detached. This is enlightenment. 99

HUANG-PO

<hr />

> 66 I have returned to the root and effort is over.
> From the first there has been no one
> to see or hear anything.
> There is nothing outside of my true home.
> Rivers quietly flow and red flowers bloom. 99

KUO-AN SHIH-YUAN

The limitless sky of meditation.
The clear moonlight of wisdom.
The truth revealed as eternal stillness.
This earth is the pure lotus-land.
This body is the body of the Buddha.

HAKUIN

When everything is seen as One,
we return to the Source
and stay where we have always been.

SENG-T'SAN

A sudden clash of thunder,
the mind-doors burst open.
and there sits old man
Buddha-nature
in all his homeliness.

CHAO-PIEN

❝ Outside no other and inside no self.
No weapon for attack or shield for defence.
I am in harmony with the wisdom of the Buddha-Way.
I walk the non-Way without abandoning ordinary life.
Appearances are flowers blooming in the sky.
Without name or form, I am beyond birth and death. ❞

P'ANG YUN

> Our Buddha-nature is there from the very beginning.
> It is like the sun emerging from behind clouds.
> It is like a mirror that reflects perfectly
> when it is wiped clean and returned to its original clarity.

HO-SHAN

The publishers would like to thank the following for the use of pictures:

e.t. archive: pp. 9, 17, 20, 27, 32, 35, 38, 53
Vanessa Fletcher: pp. 5, 13, 15, 16, 19, 21, 25, 28, 31, 37, 41, 42, 45, 48, 55, 56, 59, 60